# THE VOIDABLE TRANSACTIONS (f/k/a FRAUDULENT TRANSFER) HANDBOOK- 3d Supplement
## A Practical Guide For Lawyers and Clients

By Earl M. Forte

# THE VOIDABLE TRANSACTIONS (F/K/A FRAUDULENT TRANSFER) HANDBOOK – 3D SUPPLEMENT

by

Earl M. Forte

THE VOIDABLE TRANSACTIONS (f/k/a
FRAUDULENT TRANSFER) HANDBOOK – 3d
Supplement - A PRACTICAL GUIDE FOR LAWYERS
AND CLIENTS
Copyright © 2017 by Earl M. Forte

This is a work of non-fiction.

All rights reserved. No part of this publication may be reproduced, stored in a retrieval system, or transmitted in any form or by any means without the prior written permission of the author, nor be otherwise circulated in any form of binding or cover other than that in which it is published.

*To Paul Wohlmuth*

**Preface**

This is the 3d supplement to the original *Fraudulent Transfer Handbook,* published in 2013. First released in 2016, this supplement changes the book's title to reflect the change in title of the Uniform Fraudulent Transfer Act to the Uniform Voidable Transactions Act (the "UVTA"), which has now been enacted in fifteen states. In this 2017 re-release, I have added information regarding the six additional states that have enacted the UVTA since this supplement was first published in 2016.

VOIDABLE TRANSACTIONS (F/K/A FRAUDULENT TRANSFER) HANDBOOK – 3D SUPPLEMENT – EARL M. FORTE

## Chapter summaries for 3d supplement

1. **Continued - there is still no "fraud" in a fraudulent transfer - the Uniform Voidable Transactions Act becomes law in fifteen states.**

   Chapter 1 discusses the new Uniform Voidable Transactions Act, promulgated by the National Conference of Commissioners On Uniform State Laws in July 2014. As of this writing, it has been enacted in fifteen states and introduced for potential enactment in eight others.

2. **What they are and are not doing in the fifteen states where the UVTA has been enacted to date.**

   Chapter 2 reviews the Uniform Voidable Transactions Act, as enacted in the fifteen states that have adopted it to date – Arkansas, California, Georgia, Idaho, Indiana, Iowa, Kentucky, Michigan, Minnesota, New Mexico, North Carolina, North Dakota, Utah, Vermont and Washington. All of these states have essentially adopted the uniform version of the UVTA, however, California did not adopt the uniform provisions relating to insider preferences and series organizations. The actual statutes should be consulted for variations.

## CONTENTS
*Page*

Preface ..................................................................................... 1

Chapter summaries for 3d supplement ............................... 2

1. Continued - there is still no "fraud' in a fraudulent transfer - the Uniform Voidable Transactions Act becomes law in fifteen states............................................ 5
   a. Removal of the word "fraudulent" from the Act's title................................................................................ 7
   b. New provisions on the burden of proof ................. 9
   c. New provisions on choice of law ............................ 13
   d. Change in the definition of "insolvency" for partnerships; fair value accounting; new and different insolvency presumption ........................ 15
   e. Change in provisions regarding defenses available to transferees and obligees .................................... 18
   f. New provisions for "series" organizations ........... 20
   g. New definitions - "writing" is now "record," etc...21
   h. New and improved Official Comments ................ 22
   i. Conclusion – summary of changes ...................... 25
2. What they are and are not doing in the fifteen states where the UVTA has been enacted to date ...................... 29
   a. Arkansas ................................................................. 29
   b. California ............................................................... 30
      (1) Provisions for insider preferences not adopted.30
      (2) Provisions for series organizations not adopted.32
   c. Georgia .................................................................. 33

- d. Idaho ........................................................... 33
- e. Indiana ....................................................... 33
- f. Iowa ........................................................... 33
- g. Kentucky .................................................... 34
- h. Michigan ................................................... 34
- i. Minnesota .................................................. 34
- j. New Mexico ............................................... 35
- k. North Carolina ......................................... 35
- l. North Dakota ............................................ 35
- m. Utah .......................................................... 36
- n. Vermont .................................................... 36
- o. The UVTA has been introduced for potential enactment in eight additional states .................... 36

Table of Authorities ............................................ 37
Index ..................................................................... 41
About the author ................................................. 45

# 1.

## Continued - there is still no "fraud' in a fraudulent transfer - the Uniform Voidable Transactions Act becomes law in fifteen states.

Since the National Conference of Commissioners On Uniform State Laws (the "Commissioners" or the "Commission"), promulgated the Uniform Voidable Transactions Act (the "UVTA" or the "Act" ) in July 2014, as of this writing, it has been enacted in fifteen states and introduced for potential enactment in eight others.[1] While

---

[1] As of this writing, the UVTA has been enacted in Arkansas, California, Georgia, Idaho, Indiana, Iowa, Kentucky, Michigan, Minnesota, New Mexico, North Carolina, North Dakota, Utah, Vermont and Washington and is pending for potential enactment in Alabama, Florida, Massachusetts, New Jersey, New York, Pennsylvania, Rhode Island and South Carolina. *See,* www.uniformlaws.org/Legislative tracking. Prior to the UVTA's enactment in these fifteen states, all states (including the District of Columbia) except Alaska, Kentucky, Louisiana, Maryland, New York, South Carolina and Virginia, had

this represents significant progress toward national adoption, the UVTA is still a far cry from being as widely adopted as the UFTA, which remains the law in 30 states and the District of Columbia. At present, there appears to be little case law containing much in the way of substantive discussion of some of the newer provisions of the UVTA in the fifteen states where it has been enacted to date. *See, e.g., Luckett v. Bank of America, N.A.*, 2016 WL 193807 (Cal. App. 2016); *Martin v. Taylor*, 2016 WL 758695 (Cal. App. 2016); *In re Randall William Blanchard*, 2016 WL 806083 (Bankr. C.D. Cal. 2016); *DWC3, Inc., etc. v. Kissel*, 2016 WL 1006133 (N.C. App. 2016); *see also,* Cal. Civ. Code § 3439 *et seq.*; Idaho Code § 55-910 *et seq.*

As discussed in *The Fraudulent Transfer (a/k/a Voidable Transactions) Handbook – 2015 Supplement (revised 2017)*, while the Commissioners state that the UVTA does not propose extensive revisions to prior law under the UFTA, a number of the changes contained in the UVTA are significant and should be duly noted and studied

---

enacted the Uniform Fraudulent Transfer Act (the "UFTA") (1984). The seven states that did not enact the UFTA, relied on either the older Uniform Fraudulent Conveyance Act (the "UFCA") (1918) or a version of the Statute of 13 Elizabeth (1571). Kentucky, which had not enacted either the UFCA or the UFTA, instead relying on a version of the 446-year-old Statute of 13 Elizabeth, was one of the earliest states to move forward and enact the UVTA. As with the UFTA, states that enact the UVTA may do so with some variation from the uniform version as promulgated by the Commission. For the most part, those variations are not substantial. However, practitioners should consult local versions of the UVTA in each state to identify variations from the uniform version and to determine the UVTA's effective date in each state. *See,* Ch. 2 *infra*.

by practitioners. Following is a discussion of some of the more important changes presented by this new uniform law.

### a. Removal of the word "fraudulent" from the Act's title.

The most visible, and in this author's opinion the single most important, change proposed by the new UVTA, is the change in the Act's title – the word "fraudulent" has been dropped and replaced with the word "voidable." While the Commissioners note that this change is made solely to correct inconsistencies in the UFTA's use of the word "fraudulent" and to reduce confusion with "[n]o change in meaning...intended," this seemingly stylistic change, and all that flows from it, will have far more than mere stylistic impact and could substantially affect the way claims for voidable transactions[2] are prosecuted and tried in the courts, especially claims for so-called "actual" (a/k/a "intentional") voidable transactions. *See, UVTA,* Prefatory Notes at 6.

As noted in Chapter 1 of the original *Fraudulent Transfer Handbook* (2013 Ed.), use of the word "fraud" in the UFTA, and in the fraudulent transfer provisions of the United States Bankruptcy Code (the "Bankruptcy Code")(*see,* 11 U.S.C. § 548), is rooted in a historic misnomer, as the principal goal of voidable transactions law is not to

---

[2] As in the 2d Supplement of this book, the phrases "fraudulent transfer(s)" and "voidable transaction(s)" are used interchangeably.

compensate individual victims of fraud or to punish individual wrongdoers, but to preserve the debtor's assets for the benefit of all the debtor's general unsecured creditors. *See,* Forte, Earl M., *Fraudulent Transfer Handbook* (2013 Ed.) at 11-14. The Commissioners' decision to remove the word "fraudulent" from the Act's title is an attempt to correct this misnomer, and, as discussed below, a number of the other changes in the UVTA, such as new provisions relating to the burden of proof, flow directly from this change in the Act's title. As the Commissioners note:

> The 2014 amendments change the short title of the Act from "Uniform Fraudulent Transfer Act" to "Uniform Voidable Transactions Act." The change of title is not intended to effect any change in the meaning of the Act. The re-titling is not motivated by the substantive revisions made by the 2014 amendments, which are relatively minor. Rather, the word "fraudulent" in the original title, though sanctioned by historical usage, was a misleading description of the Act as it was originally written. Fraud is not, and never has been, a necessary element of a claim under the Act. The misleading intimation to the contrary in the original title of the Act led to confusion in the courts. *See,* e.g., § 4, Comment 10. The misleading insistence on "fraud" in the original title also contributed to the evolution of widely-used shorthand terminology that further tends to distort understanding of the provisions of the Act. Thus, several theories of recovery under the Act that

> have nothing whatever to do with fraud (or with intent of any sort) came to be widely known by the oxymoronic and confusing shorthand tag "constructive fraud." *See*, §§ 4(a)(2), 5(a). Likewise, the primordial theory of recovery under the Act, set forth in § 4(a)(1), came to be widely known by the shorthand tag "actual fraud." That shorthand is misleading, because that provision does not in fact require proof of fraudulent intent. *See*, § 4, Comment 8.

*See*, UVTA § 14, Official Comment 1. The Commissioners' effort to eliminate the "oxymoronic and confusing shorthand tag 'constructive fraud'" and the "shorthand tag 'actual fraud'" is laudable, but will result in no small change in the law.

### b. New provisions on the burden of proof.

Directly related to removal of the word "fraudulent" from the Act's title, is the addition of new provisions on the burden of proof required to prove claims under the Act. These new provisions change the standard of proof for "actual"[3] fraudulent transfer claims, from the heightened "clear and convincing" standard that many courts have borrowed from the law of common law fraud, to the

---

[3] As in prior editions of this book, the phrases "actual fraudulent transfer(s)" and "intentional fraudulent transfer(s)" are used interchangeably. Likewise, in this edition, the phrases "actual voidable transaction(s)" and "intentional voidable transaction(s)" are also used interchangeably.

"preponderance of the evidence" standard, the traditional standard of proof in most civil cases.

Section 4(a) of the UFTA and the UVTA, set forth the basic requirements for so-called "actual" and "constructive" voidable transaction claims. *See, e.g.*, Delaware Uniform Fraudulent Transfer Act, 6 Del. C. § 1304(a); California Uniform Voidable Transactions Act, Cal. Civ. Code § 3429.04 (2016); Pennsylvania Uniform Fraudulent Transfer Act, 12 Pa. C.S. § 5104; New York Debtor and Creditor Law §§ 273-276; UVTA § 4(a) . *See also*, Forte, Earl M., *The Fraudulent Transfer Handbook,* (2013 Ed.) Chapter 6 ("Constructive" vs. "intentional" fraudulent transfers).

Prior to the UVTA, most courts that had addressed the issue of the burden of proof for fraudulent transfer claims, had applied a "preponderance of the evidence" standard (the traditional standard of proof in most civil cases) to claims for "constructive" fraudulent transfers, but had adopted the more stringent "clear and convincing evidence" standard of proof for claims for "intentional" fraudulent transfers, borrowing the latter from the standard of proof traditionally applied to claims for common law fraud. Many courts also added the particularity standards for fraud claims from Rule 9(b) of the Federal Rules of Civil Procedure, as a requirement for pleading claims for "intentional" fraudulent transfers. *See*, Forte, Earl M., *The Fraudulent Transfer Handbook* (2013 Ed.) at 16 citing *Global Link Liquidating Trust, etc. v. Avantel, S.A. (In re Global Link Telecom Corp., et al.)*, 327 B.R. 711, 717-18 (Bankr. D. Del. 2005); Fed. R. Civ. P. 9(b).

In recognition of the fact that no fraudulent transfer claims, even claims for "actual" or "intentional" fraudulent transfers, require proof of common law fraud, the Commissioners added provisions to § 4(c) of the UVTA adopting the "preponderance of the evidence" standard of proof for *all* claims brought under the UVTA – claims for both "constructive" and "actual" (a/k/a "intentional") voidable transactions. *See,* UVTA at § 4(c) and Official Comment 8 ("Fraud is not a necessary element of a claim under any of those provisions…Such a transaction need not bear any resemblance to common law fraud") and Comment 10 ("proof of intent to hinder, delay or defraud a creditor under § 4(a)(1) is sufficient if made by a preponderance of the evidence. That is the standard of proof ordinarily applied in civil cases. Subsection (c) thus rejects cases that have imposed an extraordinary standard, typically 'clear and convincing evidence'").

Consistent with changes to the Act's title and the burden of proof provisions, the title of § 4 ("Transfers

Fraudulent as To Present and Future Creditors" in the current UFTA), has also been changed in the UVTA to "Transfer or Obligation Voidable As to Present or Future Creditors." *See,* UVTA at § 4. In fact, a review of the UVTA reveals that the only place where the word "fraud" (or, more accurately stated, a derivation of the word "fraud") still appears in the Act is in subsection 4(a)(1), which states that a transfer or obligation is voidable by a creditor if made by the debtor "with actual intent to hinder, delay or *defraud* any creditor of the debtor." *See,* UVTA § 4(a)(1)(emphasis added); 6 Del C. § 1304(a)(1); Cal. Civ. Code § 3439.04(a)(i); 12 Pa. C.S. § 5104(a)(i); New York Debtor and Creditor Law § 276. Hence, while under the UVTA a "voidable transaction" may involve acts of fraud by the debtor, such as the perpetration of a Ponzi scheme, there is no requirement that common law fraud be shown for a claim under the UVTA to prevail.

With respect to the Commission's decision to retain the "hinder, delay or defraud" language in the UVTA, the Commissioners note that the language "is best considered to be a single term of art describing a transaction that unacceptably contravenes norms of creditors' right. Such a transaction need not bear any resemblance to common law fraud. Thus, the Supreme Court held a given transfer voidable because it was made with intent to 'hinder, delay, or defraud' creditors, but emphasized: 'We have no thought in so holding to impute to [the debtor] a willingness to participate in conduct known to be fraudulent...[H]e acted in the genuine belief that what [he] planned was fair and lawful. Genuine the belief was, but mistaken it was also. Conduct and purpose have a quality imprinted on them by the law.'" *See*, UVTA § 4, Official Comment 8, citing *Shapiro v. Wilgus*, 287 U.S. 348, 354, 357 (1932).[4]

Thus, the UVTA provides that claims for both "constructive" and "actual" voidable transactions, are subject to the same "preponderance of the evidence" standard of proof, eliminating the more stringent "clear and convincing evidence" standard that some courts have applied to "actual" fraudulent transfer claims.[5]

### c. New provisions on choice of law.

In an apparent effort to reduce choice of law disputes in voidable transaction litigation, the UVTA contains new choice of law provisions. *See*, UVTA § 10. The new

---

[4] *See also*, Forte, Earl M., *The Fraudulent Transfer Handbook – 2014 Supplement* (2014 Ed.)(1st supp. 2017), Chapter 2, What it means to 'hinder' or 'delay' creditors – *Tronox v. Kerr-McGee*.

[5] The "preponderance of the evidence" standard of proof has also been added to § 5 of the UVTA to apply to claims brought by present creditors when the debtor receives less than reasonably equivalent value in exchange and to claims involving insider transactions. *See*, UVTA § 5 (c). The "preponderance of the evidence" standard also applies to all defenses raised under § 8 of the UVTA. *See*, UVTA §§ 8 (g), 8(h); *see also*, *infra* § 1. e at 18.

provisions apply to all claims "in the nature of a claim under this [Act]", "in other words, any claim sufficiently similar to a claim under this Act as to warrant the application of this Act's choice of law rule." *See*, UVTA § 10, Official Comment 2. Rather than simply state that the new choice of law rule applies to a "claim under this Act," the Commissioners explain that "[s]ection 10(b) could not properly have been written to apply merely to 'a claim under this Act,' for such a formulation would presuppose the applicability of the substantive provisions of this Act as in force in that jurisdiction. If a question should arise as to whether a given claim is sufficiently similar to a claim under this Act that § 10(b) should apply to it, the answer is left to judicial determination." *Id.*

Under this new choice of law provision, the law that a court will apply to a voidable transaction case is determined by the debtor's geographic location at the time of the transaction. Under this approach, an individual debtor is deemed to be geographically located at his principal place of residence, a "debtor organization" that has just one place of business is deemed to be located at that one place of business, and a debtor organization that has more than one place of business is deemed to be located at its chief executive office. *See*, UVTA § 10. This is derived from analogous choice of law provisions in § 9-301 of the Uniform Commercial Code ("UCC") and should be determined based "on authentic and sustained activity, not on the basis of manipulations employed to establish a location artificially." *See*, UVTA § 10, Official Comment 3. Determining "location" under the UVTA is "completely independent of the concept of 'center of main interests' ('COMI') as that term is used in chapter 15 of the United States Bankruptcy Code." *Id.*, Official Comment 4. On this latter point, the Commissioners note that "if the debtor is an organization, the debtor's jurisdiction of organization has no bearing on the debtor's 'location' under subsection [10](a), by contrast to the presumption in Bankruptcy Code § 1516(c)(2014) that the jurisdiction in which the debtor has its registered office (i.e., its jurisdiction of organization) is its COMI." *Id.*[6]

### d. Change in the definition of "insolvency" for partnerships; fair value accounting; new and different insolvency presumption.

Section 2(c) of the UFTA, contains a definition of "insolvency" that applies only to partnerships. *See, e.g.*, 6 Del. C. § 1302(c); *former* Cal. Civ. Code § 3439.02(b)[7]; 12 Pa.

---

[6] Section 1516(c) of the Bankruptcy Code states: "[i]n the absence of evidence to the contrary, the debtor's registered office, or habitual residence in the case of an individual, is presumed to be the center of the debtor's main interests [i.e., the COMI]." 11 U.S.C. § 1516 (c).

[7] Unless otherwise stated, references to Cal. Civ. Code § 3439 *et seq.* are to the California Uniform Voidable Transactions Act, effective in California January 1, 2016.

C.S. § 5102(c); New York Debtor and Creditor Law § 271.2. The definition takes into account the assets of general partners when making an insolvency determination. *Id.*

The Commissioners viewed this approach to an insolvency determination as making sense only if the general partners were actually liable for the debts and obligations of the partnership, which, under modern partnership statutes, they typically are not. The Commission therefore decided to drop the prior definition, seeing "no good reason to define 'insolvency' differently for a partnership than for a non-partnership whose debts are guaranteed by contract." *See,* UVTA, Prefatory Note. *See also,* Cal. Civ. Code § 3439.02.

Subsection 2(a) of the UVTA has also been re-drafted to comport more closely with "fair valuation" accounting, which is used to determine insolvency under the Bankruptcy Code pursuant to the standards of the Financial Accounting Standards Board ("FASB"). *See,* Accounting Standards Codification ¶¶ 820-10-35-17 to 18 (2014) (formerly) Statement of Financial Accounting Standards No. 157; Fair Value Measurement ¶ 15 (2006). The Commissioners note that their goal was to "make clearer that 'fair valuation' applies to debts as well as to assets [but] [n]o change in meaning is intended." *See,* UVTA § 2, Official Comment 1. The Commissioners also note, however, that the application of "fair valuation" accounting standards to the valuation of debt, which FASB requires for financial accounting purposes to reflect nonperformance, would be contrary to § 2(a) of the UVTA, the purpose of "which is to assess the risk that the debtor will not be able to satisfy its liabilities. Only in unusual circumstances would the 'fair valuation' for the purpose of subsection (a) of a liquidated debt be other than its face amount." *Id.; see also, In re Trans World Airlines, Incorporated*, 134 F. 3d 188, 191-92 (3d Cir. 1998); *In re Trans World Airlines, Incorporated*, 180 B.R. 389, 422-29 (Bankr. D. Del. 1994) (debt valued at face amount when determining debtor's insolvency in preference action). *See also,* Cal. Civ. Code § 3439.02(a).

Another significant change is additional language the Commissioners have added to subsection 2(b) specifying the effect on the burden of proof resulting from the presumption of insolvency that arises when a debtor is not generally paying its debts as they come due. *See,* UVTA § 2, Official Comments 1, 2. The effect of this new presumption is to shift the entire burden of persuasion (i.e., the burden of proof) on the issue of the debtor's insolvency to the party against whom the presumption operates – most often the defendant. This is different from the effect of presumptions generally under the Federal Rules of Evidence, which is to shift only the burden of producing evidence to rebut the presumption to the party against who the presumption operates (usually the defendant), but once such evidence is presented, the presumption disappears (hence, the nickname, "bursting bubble" presumption), leaving the ultimate burden of persuasion with the party on who it originally rested (usually the plaintiff). *Id.*; *see also*, F.R.E. 301; Cal. Civ. Code § 3439.02(b).

This new and unique insolvency presumption in the UVTA was adopted by the Commissioners "in recognition of the difficulties facing creditors when attempting to prove insolvency in the bankruptcy sense, as provided in subsection [2](a)." *See*, UVTA § 2, Official Comment 2.

### e. Change in provisions regarding defenses available to transferees and obligees.

Section 8 of the UFTA, relating to defenses available to transferees or obligees, has been partially re-drafted in the new UVTA to clarify that in order to rely on the "good faith" defense, any reasonably equivalent value given by a good faith transferee or obligee, must be given *to the debtor*. In addition, the term "subsequent transferee" has been replaced with the phrase "immediate or mediate" transferee, to conform to language in § 550(a) of the Bankruptcy Code and to make clear that the good faith defense applies to recovery of or from the transferred property or its proceeds, by levy or otherwise, as well as to an action for recovery of a money judgment. *See,* UVTA, Prefatory Note § 8 and Official Comment 2. *See also,* Cal. Civ. Code §§ 3439.08(a) and (b).

The Commissioners have also added proposed language to subsection 8(e)(2), significant for secured creditors. That subsection generally protects a transferee who acquires a debtor's interest in property as the result of enforcement by a secured creditor, "which may, but need not be, the transferee," of rights under Part 6 of Article 9 of the UCC. *See,* UVTA § 8, Official Comment 5, citing *Calaiaro v. Pittsburgh National Bank, (In re Ewing),* 33 B.R. 288 (Bankr. W.D. Pa. 1983)(sale of pledged stock held subject to avoidance under § 548 of the Bankruptcy Code), *rev'd,* 36 B.R. 476 (W.D. Pa. 1984) (transfer held not avoidable because it was deemed to have occurred more than one year before the bankruptcy petition was filed). *See also,* Cal. Civ. Code § 3439.08(e)(2).

The Commissioners are of the view that the good faith and commercial reasonableness requirements of Article 9 of the UCC "provide substantial protection to the other creditors of the debtor," but they note that "[t]he exemption afforded by subsection [8](e)(2) does not extend to acceptance of collateral in full or partial satisfaction of the obligations it secures," i.e., what is sometimes referred to as "strict foreclosure." *See*, UVTA § 8 (e)(2), Official Comment 5. This is so since "[a]n exemption for strict foreclosure is inappropriate because compliance with the rules of Article 9 relating to strict foreclosure may not sufficiently protect the interests of the debtor's other creditors if the debtor does not act to protect equity the debtor may have in the asset." *Id.*

As noted above in footnote 5, new § 8 in the UVTA also adds provisions in subsections (g) and (h) establishing uniform rules for the standard of proof that apply to all defenses under the UVTA. These provisions identify the party raising the defense as the party required to prove the defense and adopt the "preponderance of the evidence" standard for proof of all defenses under § 8. *See*, UVTA §§ 8(g) and (h), Official Comments 7 and 8; *see also*, n. 5 at 13 *supra*. *See also*, Cal. Civ. Code §§ 3439.08(f) and (g).

### f. New provisions for "series" organizations.

Section 11 of the UVTA is entirely new. It applies to so-called "series" organizations, a relatively new form of business entity "exemplified by the Uniform Statutory Trusts Entity Act §§ 401-404 (2009) and Del. Code Ann. tit. § 18-215 (2012) (pertaining to Delaware limited liability companies)." *See*, UVTA § 11, Official Comment. If the statute under which the entity is organized "permits it to divide its assets and debts among 'protected series' (however denominated), such that assets and debts of, or associated with, each 'protected series' are separated in accordance with subsections (a)(2)(ii) and (iii), and if the organization does so, then the provisions of this Act [the UVTA] apply to each 'protected series' as if it were a legal entity, regardless of whether it is considered to be a legal entity for other purposes" and regardless of the terminology actually used in the statute under which the organization has been organized. *Id.*[8]

### g. New definitions - "writing" is now "record," etc.

In recognition of technological change, references in the UFTA to "writing" have been replaced in the UVTA with the word "record." *See*, UVTA Prefatory Note and § 1(13), Official Comment 13. The UVTA defines "record" as "information that is inscribed on a tangible medium or that is stored in an electronic or other medium and is retrievable in perceivable form." *See*, UVTA § 1(13). *See also*, Cal. Civ. Code § 3439.01(k).

Several other definitions have also been added or updated and are derived from the standard definitions used

---

[8] As noted in Chapter 2 *infra*, California did not adopt the provisions from the uniform version of the UVTA that apply to series organizations. *See*, California SB 161, April 14, 2015, Uniform Fraudulent Transfer Act, Synopsis at 6.

in acts prepared by the Commissioners as of 2014, e.g., the word "electronic" has been added, a new definition of "person" (which adds non-profit entities, public corporations, "or instrumentality, or other legal entity" and is intended to include "protected series" or a "series organization," even though a "protected series" may not qualify as a "person") has been added, as has the word "sign," which means "present intent to authenticate or adopt a record." *See,* UVTA §§ 1(7), (11) and (15), Official Comments 7, 11 and 15. The UVTA also contains a new definition of "organization," derived from § 1-201(b)(25) of the UCC (2014). The new definition states that "'[o]rganization' means a person other than an individual." *See,* UVTA § 1(10). *See also,* Cal. Civ. Code §§ 3439.01(f), (h) and (l).

### h. New and improved Official Comments.

The UVTA contains new and more extensive Official Comments that improve discussion and do an excellent job explaining the Commissioners' revisions. For example, the Official Comment to definition (8) "insider," contains a new discussion emphasizing the non-exclusive nature of the types of "insiders" enumerated in the official definition and noting the unique factual nature of determining "insider" status. *See,* UVTA § 1(8), Official Comment 8.

The Official Comment to § 2, Insolvency, adds an excellent discussion of "fair value" accounting derived from the FASB rules and describes the unusual way the presumption of insolvency in § 2(b) operates – it shifts the entire burden of proof, not just the burden of producing evidence, to the party against whom the presumption operates. *See*, UVTA § 2(b), Official Comment 2. As previously noted, this differs from the traditional effect of evidentiary presumptions under Rule 301 of the Federal Rules of Evidence, which is to shift only the burden of producing evidence to rebut the presumption to the party against whom the presumption operates, but leaves the ultimate burden of proof with the party on whom it originally rested. This seemingly technical change in the insolvency presumption could have a substantial impact in civil discovery, notably on expert discovery, and the manner in which insolvency evidence is presented in the courtroom by requiring the defendant to affirmatively prove solvency (or, put another way, affirmatively disprove insolvency), not simply present evidence sufficient to rebut an insolvency presumption. This change could possibly result in an increase in expert witness expenses for defendants in voidable transaction litigation.

Some of the more interesting Official Comments in the UVTA appear in § 4. For example, there is new discussion in Official Comments 2 and 8 to § 4 addressing the adoption in certain states of laws allowing for the creation of statutory trusts or other "creditor thwarting devices" that may supersede certain provisions of the UVTA, thereby legitimizing transfers or other transactions that might otherwise violate the UVTA. *See*, UVTA § 4, Official Comments 2, 8. This brings to mind asset protection trusts and similar asset protection devices that exist in some states.[9]

The Official Comments to § 4 also discuss the Commissioners' efforts to remove language that has led to concepts from the law of common law fraud being misapplied to the law of voidable transactions, such as the application by many courts of extraordinary pleading standards and burdens of proof to claims for "actual" voidable transactions when such was never intended by the UFTA. *See*, UVTA § 4, Official Comments 8, 10; *see also*, Forte, Earl M., *The Fraudulent Transfer Handbook* (2013 Ed.), Chapter 1, There is no fraud in a fraudulent transfer. The Official Comments to § 4 also contain an excellent discussion emphasizing the point that the transfer or other

---

[9] *See, e.g.*, Nenno, Richard W., *Planning and Defending Domestic Asset-Protection Trusts* (ALI-ABA April 23-27, 2012).

transaction the plaintiff may seek to avoid need only have "hindered or delayed" unsecured creditors, not necessarily "defrauded" them, nor even placed the transferred property permanently beyond their reach, to qualify as avoidable, i.e., conduct rising to the level of "badges of fraud" is not required. *See,* UVTA § 4, Official Comment 8; see *also,* Forte, Earl M., *The Fraudulent Transfer Handbook – 2014 Supplement*, Chapter 2, What it means to 'hinder' or 'delay' creditors – *Tronox v. Kerr-McGee* (2014 Ed.).

### i. Conclusion – summary of changes.

The UVTA proposes significant revisions to the UFTA. The most important of these can be summarized as follows:

- *No more "fraud."* The UVTA removes language previously in the UFTA, that had resulted in concepts from the law of common law fraud being misapplied to the law of voidable transactions. Most notably, the word "fraudulent" has been dropped from the title of the UVTA and replaced with the word "voidable."
- *Standard of proof, pleading standards.* The UVTA adopts a uniform standard of proof for all claims and defenses. It does this by adding new provisions stating that the "preponderance

of the evidence" standard of proof applies to all claims (both "actual" and "constructive") and to all defenses raised under the Act. By doing this, the UVTA adopts the standard of proof used in most civil cases and rejects the heightened "clear and convincing evidence" standard for claims of "actual" fraud that many courts have borrowed from the law of common law fraud. The Official Comments also criticize use of extraordinary pleading standards for claims of "actual" voidable transactions derived from the "particularity" requirement for pleading common law fraud set forth in Rule 9(b) of the Federal Rules of Civil Procedure.

- *Choice of law.* New choice of law provisions have been added to the UVTA making the debtor's geographical location at the time of the transaction, the determining factor for choice of law purposes. This change rejects the "center of main interest" approach from § 1516(c) of the Bankruptcy Code and is intended to reduce choice of law disputes.
- *Partnership insolvency.* The UVTA updates the definition of "insolvency" as applied to

partnerships and conforms the various tests and measures used to determine insolvency to align more closely with the definitions and tests used for determining insolvency under the Bankruptcy Code.

- *New insolvency presumption.* Under the UVTA, when a presumption of insolvency arises because the debtor is not paying its debts as they come due, the entire burden of proof on the issue of the debtor's insolvency shifts to the party against whom the presumption operates. This is a significant change from the traditional "bursting bubble" presumption under F.R.E. 301, which shifts only the burden of going forward with evidence to rebut the presumption, but once the presumption is rebutted, the ultimate burden of proof remains on the party with whom it originally rested.

- *"Subsequent transferee."* The UVTA replaces the term "subsequent transferee" with the phrase "immediate or mediate transferee" to align language in the UVTA with language in § 550(a) of the Bankruptcy Code.

- *Debtor property obtained from a secured creditor of the debtor.* The UVTA conforms § 8(e)(2) to provisions in Part 6 of Article 9 of the UCC to protect transferees who acquire a debtor's interest in property as the result of enforcement by a secured creditor.
- *Series organizations.* The UVTA contains a new section providing that each "protected series" of a "series organization" is to be treated like a "person" for purposes of the Act, even if not treated as a "person" for other purposes.
- *Definitions, official comments.* The UVTA contains updated and improved definitions and Official Comments.

The UVTA improves current law by better distinguishing voidable transaction claims from claims for common law fraud and by modernizing other provisions of the UFTA. While enactment of the UVTA by the states does not appear to be moving quickly -- only fifteen have enacted it to date -- the law should not be controversial and should eventually be enacted by at least a majority of the states.

# 2.

**What they are and are not doing in the fifteen states where the UVTA has been enacted to date.**

Fifteen states (Arkansas, California, Georgia, Idaho, Indiana, Iowa, Kentucky, Michigan, Minnesota, New Mexico, North Carolina, North Dakota, Utah, Vermont and Washington) have enacted the UVTA since it was promulgated by the Commission in July 2014. A review of the legislation in those states concludes that most have adopted the uniform version of the UVTA with some occasional minor variations.

### a. Arkansas.

The Arkansas Uniform Voidable Transctions Act, Arkansas Code title 4, Ch.59, § 4-59-201 *et seq.*, became effective on April 7, 2017 and replaces the prior Arkansas

UFTA. The Arkansas UVTA adopted the uniform version of the UVTA.

### b. California.

The California Uniform Voidable Transactions Act (the "California UVTA"), Cal. Civ. Code § 3439 *et seq.*, was enacted in mid-2015 and became effective on January 1, 2016. *See,* Cal. Civ. Code § 3439 *et seq.* It replaces the former California UFTA, which had been the law in California since 1986. *Id.* The California UVTA adopts the uniform version of the UVTA with two significant exceptions.

#### (1) Provisions for insider preferences not adopted.

Section 5(b) of the UVTA allows for the avoidance and recovery of so-called "insider" preferences. *See,* UVTA § 5(b). An "insider" preference occurs when a transfer of the debtor's property is made to an insider, for or on account of antecedent debt, when the debtor is insolvent and when the insider had reasonable cause to believe at the time of the transfer that the debtor was insolvent. *Id.* at Official Comment 2. Subsection 5(b) is designed to adopt for general application the rule of such cases as *Jackson Sound Studios, Inc. v. Travis,* 473 F. 2d 503 (5th Cir. 1973) (security transfer of corporation's equipment to corporate principal's mother perfected on the eve of bankruptcy of the corporation was held to be voidable); *In re Lamie Chemical Co.*, 296 F. 24 (4th Cir. 1924) (corporate preference made to corporate officers who had voted for liquidation); and *Stuart v. Larson*, 298 F.223 (8th Cir. 1924) (corporate preference to director held voidable). *Id.*

With respect to the California UVTA, the State Bar Committee recommended against adopting these provisions in California "based upon the fact that the Legislature rejected the adoption of those provisions when it initially adopted the Model [UFTA] Act in 1986" and while "[f]ailure of the Legislature to adopt a provision 30 years ago is not sufficient justification for not adopting such provisions now. . .there is a better justification for not incorporating this provision into the Act [UVTA]: Section 1800(b) of the [California] Code of Civil Procedure allows an assignee to sue to recover preferential transfers. Therefore, state law already provides a venue for creditors to seek recovery for such transfers and therefore does not need to be amended to incorporate this provision from the Model Act [UVTA]." *See,* SB 161, April 14, 2015, Uniform Fraudulent Transfer Act, Synopsis at 6.

## (2) Provisions for series organizations not adopted.

Another provision from the uniform version of the UVTA that was not adopted into the California UVTA was the provision in § 11 relating to so-called "series" organizations. *See*, Forte, Earl M., *The Fraudulent Transfer (a/k/a Voidable Transactions) Handbook – 2015 Supplement (2nd supp. 2017)* at 20-21. Series organizations are a relatively new form of business entity exemplified by the Uniform Statutory Trusts Entity Act §§ 401-404 (2009) and Del. Code. Ann. tit. § 18-215 (2012). *Id. See*, UVTA § 11, Official Comment.

The State Bar of California recommended against adoption of the provisions in the uniform version of the UVTA relating to series organizations because "such adoption is premature and unnecessary", as "[s]eries organizations cannot be formed in California as a matter of law and therefore the practice of foreign series organizations transacting business in California 'doesn't appear to be common place'. . .and based upon the information available to the Committee, is premature and there is no need to develop legislation in response to a problem that does not appear to exist." *See*, SB 161, April 14, 2015, Uniform Fraudulent Transfer Act, Synopsis at 6.

c. **Georgia.**

Georgia has adopted the uniform version of the UVTA, including the provisions relating to insider preferences and series organizations. *See,* Ch. 2, Official Code of Georgia Annotated, Art. 4 § 18-2-70 *et seq.*; H.B. 197.

d. **Idaho.**

Idaho has adopted the uniform version of the UVTA, including the provisions relating to insider preferences and series organizations. *See,* Idaho Code Annotated § 55-910 *et seq.*

e. **Indiana.**

Indiana has adopted the uniform version of UVTA "in part", however, a review of the statute suggests only minor differences from the uniform version. *See* Burns Ind. Code Ann. § 32-18-2-2 *et seq.* The Indiana UVTA became effective on July 1, 2017.

f. **Iowa.**

Iowa has adopted the uniform version of the UVTA, including the provisions relating to insider preferences and series organizations. *See,* Iowa Statutes § 684.1 *et seq.*

### g. Kentucky.

Having never enacted either the UFCA (1918) or the UFTA (1984), Kentucky had relied instead on the 445-year old Statute of 13 Elizabeth, originally enacted by the British Parliament in 1571. Kentucky quickly leap-frogged into the modern era, however, when in 2015 it became one of the first states to enact the entire uniform version of the UVTA, including its provisions relating to insider preferences and series organizations. *See*, Kentucky Revised Statutes § 378A *et seq.*; *see also*, 15 RS SB 204/GA, Unofficial Copy as of 12/16/15.

### h. Michigan.

Michigan enacted the uniform version of the UVTA, which became effective there on January 6, 2017. *See* MCLS § 566.31 *et seq.*

### i. Minnesota.

With the exception of the provisions from § 9 of the uniform version of the UVTA entitled "Extinguishment of Cause of Action," Minnesota has adopted the uniform version of the UVTA, including the provisions relating to insider preferences and series organizations. Practitioners should consult other provisions of Minnesota law for the appropriate statutes of limitations for claims brought under the Minnesota UVTA. *See,* Minnesota Statutes § 513.41 *et seq.*

### j. New Mexico.

With the exception of a few non-substantive differences relating largely to formatting of the statute, and some additional provisions relating to the statute's applicability and effective date, New Mexico has adopted the uniform version of the UVTA, including its provisions relating to insider preferences and series organizations. *See,* New Mexico Statutes Annotated § 56-10-15 *et seq.*

### k. North Carolina.

With only minor, non-substantive differences, North Carolina has adopted the uniform version of the UVTA, including the provisions relating to insider preferences and series organizations. *See,* North Carolina General Statutes, 39 Article 3A § 39-23.1 *et seq.*

### l. North Dakota.

With only minor, non-substantive differences relating to the sequence in which several sections of the statute are presented, North Dakota has adopted the uniform version of the UVTA, including the provisions relating to insider preferences and series organizations. *See,* North Dakota Century Code Annotated § 13-02-01 *et seq.*

### m. Utah.

Utah enacted the uniform version of the UVTA, which became effective there on March 21, 2017. *See* Utah Code Annotated, Ch.6 § 25-6-101 *et seq.*

### n. Vermont.

Vermont enacted the uniform version of the UVTA, which became effective there on March 4, 2017. *See* 9 V.S.A., Ch.57, § 2285 *et seq.*

### o. The UVTA has been introduced for potential enactment in eight additional states.

As of this writing, the UVTA has been introduced for potential enactment in Alabama, Florida, Massachusetts, New Jersey, New York, Pennsylvania, Rhode Island and South Carolina. *See* www.uniformlaws.org. More states are expected to follow. *See, e.g., Report of The Amendments To The Fraudulent Transfer Act (To Be Known As The Pennsylvania Voidable Transactions Act)*, Pennsylvania Bar Association Quarterly, April 2015, Vol. LXXXVI, No. 2 at 83.

## TABLE OF AUTHORITIES

**Page(s)**

## Cases

*Calaiaro v. Pittsburgh National Bank, (In re Ewing),*
33 B.R. 288 (Bankr. W.D. Pa. 1983), *rev'd*, 36 B.R. 476
(W.D. Pa. 1984) ........................................................................ 19

*DWC3, Inc., etc. v. Kissel,*
2016 WL 1006133 (N.C. App. 2016) ...................................... 6

*Global Link Liquidating Trust, etc. v. Avantel, S.A. (In re Global Link Telecom Corp., et al.),*
327 B.R. 711 (Bankr. D. Del. 2005) ...................................... 11

*In re Lamie Chemical Co.,*
296 F. 24 (4$^{th}$ Cir. 1924) ..................................................... 30

*In re Randall William Blanchard,*
2016 WL 806083 (Bankr. C.D. Cal. 2016) .............................. 6

*In re Trans World Airlines, Incorporated,*
134 F. 3d 188 (3d Cir. 1998) ................................................. 17

*In re Trans World Airlines, Incorporated,*
180 B.R. 389 (Bankr. D. Del. 1994) ..................................... 17

*Jackson Sound Studios, Inc. v. Travis,*
473 F. 2d 503 (5$^{th}$ Cir. 1973) ............................................. 30

*Luckett v. Bank of America, N.A.,*
2016 WL 193807 (Cal. App. 2016) ......................................... 6

*Martin v. Taylor,*
2016 WL 758695 (Cal. App. 2016) ......................................... 6

*Shapiro v. Wilgus*,
287 U.S. 348 (1932) ................................................................. 13

*Stuart v. Larson*,
298 F.223 (8th Cir. 1924) ........................................................ 31

## Statutes

11 United States Code § 1516 ................................................. 15

11 United States Code § 548 ..................................................... 7

Arkansas Uniform Voidable Transctions Act, Arkansas
Code title 4, Ch.59, § 4-59-201 *et seq.* ................................... 29

California Civil Code § 3439 *et seq.* ................................ passim

California Uniform Voidable Transactions Act, Cal. Civ.
Code § 3429 *et seq* (2016) ............................................... passim

Ch. 2, Official Code of Georgia Annotated, Art. 4 § 18-2-
70 *et seq.* .............................................................................. 32

Del. Code Ann. tit. § 18-215 (2012) .................................. 20, 32

Delaware Uniform Fraudulent Transfer Act, 6 Del. C. §
1304(a) ................................................................ 10, 12, 15, 17

Idaho Uniform Voidable Transactions Act, Idaho Code §
55-910 *et seq.* ..................................................................... 6, 33

Indiana Uniform Voidable Transactions Act, Burns Ind.
Code Ann. § 32-18-2-2 *et seq.* ............................................... 33

Iowa Uniform Voidable Transactions Act, Iowa Statutes §
684.1 *et seq.* ........................................................................... 33

Kentucky Uniform Voidable Transactions Act, Kentucky
Revised Statutes § 378A *et seq.* ............................................. 34

Michigan Compiled Laws and Statutes § 566.31 *et seq.* ............. 34

Minnesota Uniform Voidable Transactions Act, Minnesota Statutes § 513.41 et seq. .............................................................. 34

New Mexico Uniform Voidable Transactions Act, New Mexico Statutes Annotated § 56-10-15 et seq. ........................ 35

New York Uniforms Fraudulent Conveyance Act, New York Debtor and Creditor Law § 270 et seq ................. 10, 12, 15

North Carolina Uniform Voidable Transactions Act, North Carolina General Statutes, 39 Article 3A § 39-23.1 et seq. ..................................................................................................... 35

North Dakota Uniform Voidable Transactions Act, North Dakota Century Code Annotated § 13-02-01 et seq. ................ 35

Pennsylvania Uniform Fraudulent Transfer Act, 12 Pa. C.S. § 5104 ............................................................................... 10, 12, 15

Uniform Statutory Trusts Entity Act §§ 401-404 (2009) ........ 20, 32

Uniform Voidable Transactions Act ........................................ passim

United States Bankruptcy Code ................................................. 7, 15

Utah Uniform Voidable Transactions Act, Utah Code Annotated, Ch.6 § 25-6-101 et seq. ............................................ 35

Vermont Uniform Voidable Transactions Act, 9 Vermont Statutes Annotated, Ch.57, § 2285 et seq. .................................. 36

## Rules

Federal Rules of Civil Procedure 9(b) ........................................... 11

Federal Rules of Evidence 301 ............................................... 18, 23

## Other Authorities

Forte, Earl M., *The Fraudulent Transfer (a/k/a Voidable Transactions) Handbook – 2015 Supplement (2nd supp. 2017)* .................................................................................... 6, 32

Forte, Earl M., *The Fraudulent Transfer Handbook – 2014 Supplement* (2014 Ed.) .......................................................... 13, 24

Forte, Earl M., *The Fraudulent Transfer Handbook* (2013 Ed.) ................................................................................ passim

Nenno, Richard W., *Planning and Defending Domestic Asset-Protection Trusts* (ALI-ABA April 23-27, 2012) ......... 24

*Report of The Amendments To The Fraudulent Transfer Act (To Be Known As The Pennsylvania Voidable Transactions Act)*, Pennsylvania Bar Association Quarterly, April 2015, Vol. LXXXVI, No. 2 at 83 .................. 36

Website of the National Conference of Commissioners on Uniform State Laws, www.uniformlaws.org ....................... 5, 36

## INDEX

2014 Supplement, 13, 24
Act, 5, 7, 8, 9, 11, 12, 14, 15, 20, 25, 27, 30, 31, 32, 36
actual, 9, 10, 11, 12, 13, 24, 25
actual fraud, 9
actual fraudulent transfer, 9
actual or intentional fraudulent transfers, 11
actual voidable transactions, 24
actual, intentional voidable transactions, 7
Article 9, 19, 27
Article 9 of the UCC, 19
badges of fraud, 24
Bankruptcy Code, 7, 15, 16, 18, 19, 26, 27
burden of persuasion, 17, 18
burden of proof, 8, 9, 10, 11, 17, 22, 23, 26, 27
bursting bubble presumption, 18, 27
California, 2, 5, 10, 15, 21, 29, 30, 31, 32, 45
California Uniform Voidable Transactions Act, 10
center of main interests, 15
choice of law, 13, 14, 26

clear and convincing, 9, 10, 11, 13, 25
COMI, 15
Commission, 5, 6, 12, 16, 29
Commissioners, 2, 5, 6, 7, 8, 9, 11, 12, 14, 15, 16, 17, 18, 19, 21, 22, 24
common law fraud, 9, 11, 12, 25, 28
confusing shorthand tag constructive fraud, 9
confusion in the courts, 8
constructive, 10
constructive and actual voidable transactions, 13
constructive fraud, 9
contravenes norms of creditors' right, 12
creditor thwarting devices, 23
debtor's geographic location, 14
defenses, 13, 18, 20, 25
Delaware limited liability companies, 20
Delaware Uniform Fraudulent Transfer Act, 10
District of Columbia, 6
*Domestic Asset-Protection Trusts*, 24

electronic, 21
fair valuation, 16
fair value accounting, 15
Fair Value Measurement, 16
Federal Rules of Civil Procedure, 26
Federal Rules of Evidence, 17
Financial Accounting Standards Board, 16
Forte, Earl M., 8, 10, 11, 13, 24, 31
Forte, Earl M., *Fraudulent Transfer Handbook*, 8
fraud, 7, 8, 9, 10, 11, 12, 24, 25
fraudulent transfer, 7
*Fraudulent Transfer Handbook*, 1
*Fraudulent Transfer Handbook* (2013 Ed.), 7, 11, 24
general partners, 15, 16
Georgia, 2, 5, 29, 32
good faith, 18, 19
good faith defense, 18
hinder, delay or defraud, 11, 12
hinder, delay, or defraud, 12
Idaho, 2, 5, 6, 29, 33
immediate or mediate transferee, 18
insider, 22
insider preferences, 2, 30, 32, 33, 35
insolvency, 15, 16, 17, 18, 22, 23, 26
insolvency determination, 15, 16
insolvency for partnerships, 15
insolvency presumption, 15, 23, 26
intentional fraudulent transfers, 10, 11
Iowa, 2, 5, 29, 33
jurisdiction, 14, 15
Kentucky, 2, 5, 29, 33
location under the UVTA, 15
Minnesota, 2, 5, 29, 34
misnomer, 7
National Conference of Commissioners On Uniform State Laws, 2, 5
new definitions, 21
New Mexico, 2, 5, 29, 34
New York Debtor and Creditor Law, 10, 12, 15
nine states, 2, 29
North Carolina, 2, 5, 29, 35
North Dakota, 2, 5, 29, 35
obligation, 12

Official Comment, 9, 11, 13, 14, 15, 16, 18, 19, 20, 21, 22, 24, 30, 32
organization, 22
particularity standards, 10
Pennsylvania Uniform Fraudulent Transfer Act, 10
person, 21, 27
Ponzi scheme, 12
preponderance of the evidence, 10, 11, 13, 20, 25
Present or Future Creditors, 12
preserve the debtor's assets, 8
presumption, 15, 17, 18, 22
presumptions, 17, 23
protected series, 20, 21, 27
reasonably equivalent value, 13, 18
record, 21, 22
Removal of the word fraudulent, 7
remove the word fraudulent, 8
Rule 301 of the Federal Rules of Evidence, 23
Rule 9(b) of the Federal Rules of Civil Procedure, 10
secured creditors, 19

series organizations, 2, 20, 27, 31, 32, 34, 35
shift only the burden of producing evidence, 17, 23
shorthand tag actual fraud, 9
sign, 22
standard of proof, 9, 10, 11, 13, 20, 25
State Bar of California, 32
states, 6, 23, 28
Statute of 13 Elizabeth, 6, 33
statutory trusts, 23
strict foreclosure, 19
subsequent transferee, 18, 27
Supreme Court, 12
*The Fraudulent Transfer (a/k/a Voidable Transactions) Handbook – 2015 Supplement*, 6, 32
*Trans World Airlines*, 17
transferred property, 18
*Tronox v. Kerr-McGee*, 13, 24
UCC, 14, 19, 22, 27
UFCA, 6, 33
UFTA, 6, 7, 10, 12, 15, 18, 21, 24, 25, 28
Uniform Commercial Code, 14

Uniform Fraudulent Conveyance Act, 6
Uniform Fraudulent Transfer Act, 1, 6, 8, 10, 21, 31, 32
Uniform Statutory Trusts Entity Act, 20
Uniform Voidable Transactions Act, 1, 2, 5, 8
United States Bankruptcy Code, 7, 15
UVTA, 2, 5, 6, 7, 8, 9, 10, 11, 12, 13, 14, 16, 17, 18, 19, 20, 21, 22, 23, 24, 25, 26, 27, 28, 29, 30, 31, 32, 33, 34, 35, 36
valuation of debt, 16
Voidable, 12
voidable transactions, 7, 11, 24, 25, 26

## About the author

Earl M. Forte is a partner at the law firm of Eckert Seamans Cherin & Mellott, LLC and is a member of the firm's Litigation and Business Counseling groups. He has substantial experience in corporate litigation, bankruptcy and other insolvency and business matters, including fraudulent transfer matters. Mr. Forte has been practicing law enthusiastically for over 30 years and represents a variety of clients. This is the third supplement to Mr. Forte's book, *The Fraudulent Transfer Handbook*, originally published in 2013. See www.amazon.com. More information about Mr. Forte and his law firm Eckert Seamans is available at Eckert Seaman's website www.eckertseamans.com.

www.ingramcontent.com/pod-product-compliance
Lightning Source LLC
Chambersburg PA
CBHW031502210526
45463CB00003B/1038